I'VE MADE PLANS

A MEMOIR OF REBUILDING

MIA J HANKS

DIVINE DESTINY PUBLISHING

For Aunt Mary

"You don't have to see the whole staircase, just take the first step." — Martin Luther King Jr.

CONTENTS

AUTHOR'S NOTE

In 2024 I published my first book, *Bride-Made: A Memoir*, an account of my life with a covert narcissistic husband. While organizing chapters for the memoir, I shared one particular story with my Aunt Mary. Mary was an author herself with two published books at the time. She was also the most faith-based person I knew, and I thought she would be interested to read this particular short chapter. It was a quiet account of my faith journey, a story I called "Tripods." Mary read my piece and loved this story of how God had led me during my divorce. She told me to make sure to include this vignette in my upcoming debut book. She felt it was not only my story to tell, but a story that others needed to hear.

When *Bride-Made* came together as a final manuscript, my Tripod story simply had nowhere to land. It just felt out of rhythm with the pace of the book. Because of its awkwardness, I chose to let it go. I knew how much my aunt had hoped this chapter would be included, and I promised myself that if I ever wrote another book, I would do my best to find a home for the story of the tripods. That promise would ultimately guide me into my next venture as a writer.

After *Bride-Made* was published I kept feeling a tug to write again, but I was unsure of the direction I should go. I had already told the account of my courtship, my marriage and the unravelling that followed. I wasn't sure there was anything left to say. However, I realized that healing was a big part of my life, just as my marriage had been, and a new book could answer the question that lingered- After the divorce, then what?

In 2025 my Aunt Mary passed away at the age of 99. A few months after her passing I definitively decided to continue my story with *I've Made Plans*, and this time I decided to carve out a space for the chapter that had earlier been set aside. This faith-based testimony ultimately found its way into the final pages of my new book. I would like to believe that my Aunt Mary is proud, knowing that I can now finally share the story she asked me to tell.

INTRODUCTION

When I was twenty-one years old, I walked down the aisle of a small church. I had dreams of what my life would be as a new bride. I had my entire future planned. We said "I do" to one another, and I became a wife to my twenty-three-year-old college sweetheart. It was a promise of marital bliss, and a beautiful dream shared. What I did not know, however, was that I was stepping into a carefully crafted nightmare. The man standing next to me, my new husband, who looked like the answer to all my prayers, was a narcissist. That day would be the start of a long and disorienting journey that would have a few ups, but far too many downs. I found myself often thinking, "How did I end up here?" "Why did I not see it before I made this life-altering decision?" "How could I have been so easily deceived?" I asked myself these questions for nearly three decades. But most importantly I asked, "Why did I stay?" That burning question ate a hole in me, making me question my own intelligence, my own self-worth and my own sanity.

There are so many reasons why victims of narcissists remain victims for years, for decades, and sometimes for life. There is the financial abuse, the gaslighting, the manipulation, fear of sharing custody of children, and so on. Perhaps, though, the biggest reason I stayed stuck for so long was simply due to complacency. I became a master at sweeping things under the rug, so to speak. Big things were reasoned away, and little things just didn't matter, and so I swept. I began to make excuses for him. It was just a bad day, or my husband was stressed out due to his job, or what I often did just to keep the peace- say it was all my fault. I spent every day in the hope-draining, revolving wheel of convincing myself tomorrow would be better. The little things remained little…until they weren't. This build up happens so easily, too easily as a matter of fact, and it slowly tears down who you are.

Have you ever gone grocery shopping and thought you'd pick up just a few things? Two or three items are all that you need, so you think it will just be a quick trip to the store. Walking up and down the aisles, you find a few more goods that you didn't think you needed, but you suddenly decide they are necessities. So, you add them to your cart. Then a few more odds and ends make their way onto the pile. The addition of a few snacks that look especially tasty, and maybe a magazine or two, and before you know it your cart is getting more stocked than you initially anticipated. A couple more aisles yield even a few more items you didn't intend to buy at the start of this shopping trip. Finally, you arrive at the check-out. Your cart is full, completely full, and you wonder to yourself, "How did I end up with so much stuff?" You had come to the store to buy a few items and now your cart is overflowing. Your bill is much higher than expected. You didn't come to the store prepared to spend so much money.

This is exactly how victims can end up in decades long relationships and marriages with narcissistic partners. By ignoring the "little things," and pushing your cart along, you become complacent with the abuse that is consuming you. Then one day when you arrive at that checkout counter with too many items, and you ask yourself, "How did I get here?" At the end of my 29-year marriage this is exactly what my inquisitive mind was wondering. The culmination of years of emotional abuse and manipulation had left me completely broken. I had become a different person, one that I no longer recognized. I had lost myself while wandering up and down those aisles, placing more and more into my cart. The little things had now become the big things, and I had reached a breaking point. I had overspent myself, and now there was nothing left of me. Rather than face the embarrassment of getting out of line and returning the items in my cart back onto the shelf, I just paid the cost. That cost was one that was incredibly hard to manage, but it had to be paid to avoid admitting there was a problem.

Ultimately, my life took a dramatic and necessary turn. My cart had overflowed and overturned. Everything that had been built fell apart. Divorce. All my plans, my dreams, the future of wedded bliss I had pictured in my mind, were gone. My plans hadn't just gone awry, they had been burned to ash. Today, I am rebuilding. After 29 years of marriage to a narcissist I made the decision to start over from scratch and venture into the great unknown. There would be so much healing to do and so many truths to face. My life became exciting and terrifying all at the same time, but this was a journey that I would not regret taking.

Today I'm facing a whole new world with new adventures and lots of twists and turns. I'm discovering new things about myself and the world around me every single day. A few of the truths I've learned so far on my journey include:

Intimidation cannot rule me.

I am worthy of good things.

I can let go of what is not meant for me.

My family is not broken.

Self-isolation is not healthy.

I am more capable that I imagined.

Self-care is not selfish.

Boundaries are necessary.

Small mistakes aren't the end of the world.

Freedom is priceless.

I can face my biggest fears.

My faith sustains me.

These facts have laid the groundwork for this new life that I am rebuilding. It's a life that is full of unknown opportunities and so much promise. The plans I had originally made required me to give up being myself for my narcissistic husband. Today, my plans are letting me be me. My story didn't end with my divorce. In fact, I'm pretty sure my story is just getting started.

1

CASE CLOSED

"Divorce isn't such a tragedy. A tragedy's staying in an unhappy marriage, teaching your children the wrong things about love. Nobody ever died of divorce."

— Jennifer Weiner, Fly Away Home

I arrived at the courthouse about an hour early and made my way into a bustling courtroom. This wasn't just any courtroom. It was the place where marriages go to die. I was prepared to come face to face with the man who would officially, and not a moment too soon, become my ex-husband. No fewer than a dozen embittered couples were waiting their turn to stand before a very impatient and unforgiving divorce court judge. He was running a no-nonsense operation. He expected 100 percent preparedness, and he was quick to send away anyone who was unorganized and those who dared to show up with missing paperwork. Fortunately, my lawyer had my documents ready to go, and when it was my turn, I confidently walked forward, never making eye contact with my husband who stood with a smirk on his face. Though invisible, the tension in the air was heavy as we stood only a few feet apart. We were here merely for a signature to make our divorce final, not for confrontation but instead, for conclusion. The back and forth, contentious arguing and dividing of assets had taken place two weeks earlier in a mediation session, and today was the day to seal the deal and make this divorce official.

My ex, myself, and our lawyers would spend only about five strained minutes standing before this judge. The quick session would require elementary answers to just a few basic questions. I verified my name and stated how long I had been married. Yes, we have two children, neither of whom are minors. Yes, I consent to this divorce and yes, I am of sound mind and body. Then came a question, the final question, that halted me in my tracks. I had been schooled by my attorney a few days prior on all of these questions, so I was prepared for this humdinger. Still, it gave me pause.

"Have you and your spouse reached a fair agreement on the division of your marital assets?"

The judge awaited my answer. I was supposed to say yes, but suddenly all of my confidence escaped me. I had to say yes in order to move this divorce along, but the word simply did not want to form on my lips.

My husband is a covert narcissist. After 29 difficult years I had walked away. I was finished. The emotional and psychological abuse had become too hard to bear, and life with this man was no longer sustainable. I had to get out in order to save myself. Even so, the decision had been a difficult one. Nearly three decades earlier I had recited the marriage vows,

"Til death do us part." I took my vows seriously and I struggled with guilt about breaking these vows. I would be fracturing my family and causing such a rift in our lives. My husband had made sure to remind me of this often throughout our separation period.

It had taken me many months, but I finally began to realize that my marriage vows had already been broken. Those vows had been broken years before my departure, years before I even had the inclination to leave. They had been broken slowly, repeatedly and completely by my husband. He was the one who had truly been the demise to our relationship. As part of our vows, we had promised to "love, honor and cherish." My husband had not done any of these things. He had, in actuality, replaced these words with "manipulate, abuse and intimidate." Our vows had been severed years prior, when love had become something I had to survive.

Covert narcissism is a tricky thing to navigate, especially when its victims are unaware that this personality disorder even exists. This was me- completely unaware. While most people think all narcissists are arrogant, pompous, and overconfident, this definition fails to describe the covert type. As a covert, my husband was kind and generous to the outside world. He was a completely different person behind closed doors- thus the term "covert." The world saw an empathetic, caring, nice guy, and my family saw someone who controlled, manipulated, verbally abused and intimidated on a daily basis. Two starkly different people. The nice guy was just a farce. The abuser lived under my roof.

Upon leaving my husband I quickly learned that narcissists do not take no for an answer. They do not allow discarding. They have to win, and they will win at every turn, no matter what they have to do to make it so. My narcissistic husband had been out for revenge since the day he learned I was not coming back to him. His love bombing and fake promises weren't going to work this time. He was not going to win me back, and he was astounded. In his mind he had been victimized. How dare I walk out on him, and how dare I mar his reputation. And so began the manipulation and moving around of assets. He would make sure, if it was the last thing he did on earth, that I would not get my fair share of our marital property. He was successful in this endeavor, too, thanks to a high-power team of minions working to gain his approval and, of course, their due payment.

I wanted to fight my narcissistic husband for my fair share of our marital assets, but I quickly saw that this fight would get me nowhere It was a dead end. My legal team was able to eke out enough to give me a very comfortable life, and in the end, it was decided that I should take his offer. Was it fair? Considering the abuse I had endured for nearly three decades, absolutely not. But my only other option involved more legal fees, more time, a battle in court, calling witnesses and the like. The stress this elongated process would cause simply wasn't worth it, especially given that there was no guarantee of a larger settlement.

At the end of the day, divorce mediation revolves around nothing but a calculator. Twenty-nine years of marriage and years of abuse and trauma all came down to a simple math equation. Punch in the numbers and arrive at a settlement. No emotion, no feelings, just a cold, harsh number. At the end of our 10-hour mediation I had begrudgingly agreed to my husband's terms. Taking his offer was somewhat painful but it would put a lid on our marriage, and I needed out. I needed this to be over.

Two weeks later, standing before the judge, all eyes were on me. I was expected to answer the question affirmatively.

"Have you and your spouse reached a fair agreement on the division of your marital assets?"

Quietly, with markedly less confidence than I showed when I initially approached the bench, I paused for a second and then said, "Um, yes." With that final word uttered from my mouth, the judge took his pen and signed his name on the decree. There was no spectacle, just a quiet pen stroke that would completely rearrange my life in an instant. Twenty-nine years of marriage ended without a ceremony. I would leave the courtroom the recipient of an unfair settlement and the proud owner of a new life. With that simple signature, the manipulation and control that I had lived under for nearly three decades would end. My future now belonged to me.

2

STORAGE WARS

"The louder the threat, the smaller the man"

— Unknown

INTIMIDATION CANNOT RULE ME.

My divorce was finalized, over, complete. My marriage now ceased to exist. As part of the divorce decree, I had been awarded the contents of a storage unit. With our children getting older, my ex-husband and I had made the decision to downsize our home in the months prior to my departure. We had sold our house and moved into an apartment temporarily while we were house hunting. We had sold much of our furniture in this transition process and placed what was left in storage. A few days after the decree had been signed, I made a trip over to the storage facility to evaluate what was there and determine what I would keep and what I might sell.

Upon arriving at my unit and placing my key in the lock I was surprised when the key wouldn't turn. I tried the remaining keys on my keychain, knowing already that none of them would fit this particular lock. Not surprisingly, none of the keys would budge. Once again, I tried the key that I knew was correct and once it again there was no motion. I happened to look down at the ground as I was trying to force this key, and I saw something that caught my eye. It was a small pile of silver shards, metal-like, very finely ground up and lying in a pile directly under the lock. In that moment I knew exactly what had happened and why my key refused to work.

I made my way to the office and spoke with the man at the front desk, who incidentally happened to be the manager of the facility. Was he aware that the lock on my unit had been cut? His answers were vague at best.

"I don't think so, but I can't say for certain," the man stated.

When I questioned him further and asked if HE had cut the lock, I got another wishy-washy answer.

"I might have, but I don't really remember."

He checked the computer system and verified that the storage unit did in fact belong to me, and only me. While the contents of the unit belonged to both me and my husband during our marriage, the name on the unit had always been mine and mine alone. No question about it. I made the decision to have the lock cut. It would be the only way to gain entrance into my storage unit, and fortunately the man obliged with no argument whatsoever. While he didn't want to make any confessions, this was clearly the second time he would be cutting this lock. He proceeded to follow me to my unit with some sort of bolt cutting mechanism and after about five minutes of loud screeching and flying orange-colored sparks, I was able to gain access to my unit.

I opened the large rolling door, and upon careful examination I noted that only one item was definitely missing. It was a desk. This was a family heirloom of my ex-husband's. It had belonged to his late father, and this was something that I had most definitely planned to return to him. In fact, it was going to be my first order of business when I inventoried the contents of the storage unit. Turns out, however, he had beat me to it. He had come into the facility and more likely than not, he had paid the man at the desk to cut the lock for him. Money talks, and my ex's money spoke loudly that day. He had clearly entered the unit, took his desk, placed a new lock on the unit and then took the new key with him. This left me zero access to my storage unit. Why didn't he just ask me for access to the unit? Or why didn't he make a request through our attorneys to acquire his desk? The answer is simple-intimidation.

Narcissists are notorious for using intimidation tactics and my ex was no exception. He wanted to make a statement. He wanted to let me know that he will enter wherever he pleases and take whatever he wants. He believes definitively that it is his right, that he is special, and that he doesn't require permission. In his mind he doesn't need to go through the necessary channels to make things work for him. He does as he wishes, and the world complies.

My narcissistic ex-husband didn't bother to clean up those ground up slivers of metal on the concrete floor. Perhaps he wanted me to see them. He wanted me to know that he had been there. He had left his calling card, and his intent was likely to scare and intimidate me. Even though we were now legally divorced he still felt a need to exercise control, to induce fear and to let me know he was still the boss, at least in his mind he was.

In my marriage, I was beholden to my husband's fear and intimidation tactics. I caved every time and made sure he got his way, and this is something that I am embarrassed to admit now. However, at the time it was a coping mechanism. It was easier to keep the peace than to create conflict, so I went along to get along. On this day, however, things were much different. I didn't have to gain his approval. I didn't have to appease him or walk on eggshells or worry that I would trigger him, which could result in a terrifying angry outburst. It was no longer necessary to feed his ego, and I realized then and there that I should no longer need to feel intimidated by him or his actions.

Letting go of the feelings of fear and intimidation after a toxic relationship can be challenging. Victims are so ingrained to feel these emotions in their daily lives. As participants in these partnerships with narcissistic or toxic significant others, we learn to observe the proverbial weather patterns, watching for storm clouds. Hyper vigilance becomes a way of life. We watch for the impending storms and prepare for the worst. As a survivor of narcissistic abuse, I had to begin to learn that my ex-husband's intimidation and bullying could no longer impact me in the way that it once could. I no longer needed to be a storm watcher. I had unattached myself from him and now I was living my own life. It was time to let go of the fear that had controlled me for far too long.

Switching gears from fearful and intimidated to fearless and confident is a gradual process, and it certainly wouldn't happen overnight for me. In order to shed these feelings, it is pertinent that I felt safe, and safe was not an emotion that was prevalent for me in my marriage. My brain had been wired for survival mode, and it definitely takes time and patience to unwind this type of thinking. Over time I would learn that these feelings of perceived danger and lack of confidence didn't have a place in my world, and I would eventually learn that I was now safe, especially now that this narcissistic man was out of my life.

My ex-husband's stunt at the storage facility, while meant to intimidate me, later made me laugh. He had most likely shelled out some cash, perhaps a lot of cash, in order to force his way into my unit, when he could have entered for free if he had simply asked me. The ridiculousness of his actions made me shake my head. He now had his desk, but I had something far more satisfying, the only key to the new lock.

Journal Prompt:

What are some specific situations or tasks that are intimidating me today and why?

3

CIRCUS PEANUTS

"Candy: Because adulting is hard." — Unknown

I AM WORTHY OF GOOD THINGS.

In the early days of my heavily contentious divorce proceedings, I found myself struggling to find any semblance of happiness or peace. Filing the divorce papers had been a scary experience for me, and fear of the unknown was plaguing me. I feared retaliation from my soon to be ex-husband, and this left me feeling somewhat anxious. I didn't have any prior experience in this department and stepping into such a malicious break-up felt overwhelming. Being the narcissist that he is, this divorce would be my ex-husband's grand finale of cruelness. He was going to fight me tooth and nail at every single turn. Nothing about this dissolution of our marriage would be easy or fun. It would be a fight to the finish, and a long one at that taking just under a year.

About a month into this battle, a close, longtime friend of mine, who had been privy to all of the drama, was pained from watching my mental health suffer under the weight of the stress. Always the creative one with an uncanny knack at analogies and a mind that seemed to bend problems into solutions easily, he decided to offer some help. He devised a very innovative plan, one that would make perfect sense to me.

One day a large white box arrived at my doorstep. It was a welcomed surprise, but I was puzzled to see there was no return address. I carefully opened it and peeked in to see what was inside. After one quick glance, I immediately knew who this package was from. I turned the box upside down and proceeded to empty out an array of all my favorite candies, a bag of black jellybeans, Cadbury Creme Eggs and the elusive Cherry Mash, just to name a few. That wasn't all, however. At the bottom of the box was a bag of circus peanuts- the spongy, peanut shaped marshmallow candy that seems to inspire universal disdain. Most people agree this is the worst tasting candy in America. But me? I make no apologies. I'm not ashamed to admit that I love these things with their banana-flavored sweetness.

I immediately jumped on a Skype call with my friend and thanked him for such a kind gesture. It really, truly had made my day and he was happy that I was happy for a change. Then he said to me, "Take a look at the bag of circus peanuts." I was a little confused, but I carefully examined the bag. My friend continued, "You know, you are probably the only person in America who actually likes these things." I laughed and said, "True!" My friend went on to explain, "When you find circus peanuts in the store, oftentimes they are hard and stale. That's because no one buys them but you…" Again, I laughed, and he continued. “I had to go to three stores to find a bag of fresh, squishy circus peanuts.” I was somewhat shocked by this, feeling a little bad that he had gone to that much trouble for a silly bag of candy. He then said, “I did this to illustrate a point to you.”

My friend went on to explain that clearly I had been conditioned in my marriage to accept the bare minimum. He was exactly right. This had made me overly appreciative to ANY kind gesture, no matter how big or small. My friend continued, “You should not be surprised that I put in the extra effort to finding fresh, squishy circus peanuts. Instead, you should expect it.” He explained to me that as I begin this new chapter of healing, I must start holding people to a higher standard. No more bare minimum. “You need to know your worth,” he said, “And YOU are worth more than stale circus peanuts.”

My friend was correct. I was overzealous at any kind gesture from anyone. I had spent so many years relishing in those moments when there was peace, moments when my husband had found it in his heart to be kind, even for just a day. I spent so much of my marriage waiting for the bad to come, so much so that I had a hard time enjoying the good moments. The other shoe would inevitably drop, and things would eventually fall apart. It became a routine, a vicious cycle that seemed to dictate every single day of my life. It became almost impossible to expect kindness for more than a few fleeting moments, but the truth was that I needed to raise the bar, and I needed to raise it much higher.

As victims of domestic abuse, it is easy to accept the "breadcrumb" moments. We take the smallest amount of acceptable treatment from our abusers, and we tell ourselves that is all we deserve. Victims are often told they aren't worthy of kindness and that they deserve the abuse. In his own way, my husband told me this everyday through his actions and sometimes even through his words. I never considered the idea of holding my husband to a higher standard or expecting more from him. Instead, I accepted what he gave me. I never asked for more kindness, more good days, or more empathy. Never mind asking for it. I should have expected it. I neither asked nor expected though because I new he wouldn't give it to me. And so, I settled. I lowered the bar. I lowered my expectations. Somehow, I became okay with this, and it became my normal.

Looking back now I cannot believe I accepted such subpar treatment, but I believe this has been part of my healing, having the ability to shift my focus back into the past and recognize that my reasoning was filled with all sorts of errors. I now realize I was allowing less than acceptable behavior from my husband. My bar was as low as it could have possibly been.

Healing can only truly begin when you are forced to recognize your value. Setting a higher standard through quiet recalibration and not accepting mistreatment must be the goal. You are worth more than the bare minimum of someone's effort. Good treatment should not be something that has to be earned. Instead, it should be the baseline, it should be expected. You are worth more than breadcrumbs. And if in fact you are one of these seemingly rare people who enjoy this odd, iconic candy, you too deserve the freshest, squishiest circus peanuts that can be found. Know your worth.

Journal Prompt:

In what areas of my life have I lowered the bar and what steps can I take to raise it higher?

4

SMEAR CAMPAIGN

"A rumor can travel halfway around the world while the truth is putting on its shoes." — Mark Twain

---

I CAN LET GO OF WHAT IS NOT MEANT FOR ME.

In the last few months of my marriage, I had done a lot of reading and had spent a lot of time trying to educate myself on narcissistic personality disorder. Going into the divorce process I thought I had a pretty good idea of what I could expect. After all, divorcing a narcissist is not like divorcing a neuro typical person. Dealing with an actual personality disorder that is woven into every fiber of an individual can present a whole new set of surprising issues. Two words that I had read about in all of my studying kept coming up over and over again, smear campaign.

Smear campaigns are quite common in a breakup with a narcissist. Narcissistic people feel the need to manipulate the narrative, protect their image, and be the most important and impressive person in the room. In the face of a breakup or discernment, narcissists will swiftly move to action, and my husband was no exception. He needed to spread the news far and wide, as quickly as he could. He needed to let people know that he was not the problem. He didn't cause the demise of the marriage, and nothing could possibly be his fault. He was the good guy in the equation. The problem was, I wasn't prepared for this version of the story, and I didn't think in a million years he would launch such a malignant and bitter attack on me.

While I was figuring out how my new life post-divorce was going to work, my husband was talking to people. And talking and talking and talking. Unbeknownst to me, he was telling friends and family how he had been victimized, how he had been abandoned and had been treated so unfairly. Most likely, and in true narcissistic fashion, he was projecting his bad qualities onto me. He likely accused me of being controlling, manipulative, uncaring, and so on. I'll never know specifically what he said to all of these individuals (and I probably don't want to know), but his story must have been convincing.

It wasn't long after my filing the divorce papers that "friends" started dropping out of sight. People I used to talk to on a somewhat regular basis suddenly disappeared. No one wanted to have lunch or chat. Even the number of my Facebook friends decreased. I was apparently being "un-friended' by people who had heard my husband's spiel. I was at a loss for words.

Narcissists are notorious for this thing called projection. Projection is basically a defense mechanism where the narcissist will project their own flaws, bad behaviors and shortcomings onto another person. In my husband's case that somebody was me. He was blame-shifting. In his mind there was no way in the world that he could have done anything that would warrant my departure. It was all on me. In his twisted-up world, I was the abuser. This was the ultimate projection tactic, and this, perhaps, is why my so-called friends vanished into thin air, without a trace. No one wants to support the abuser, and these people assumed that abuser was me. Could I really blame them? Yes and no.

We all know there are two sides to every story, but the problem I was facing was that no one wanted to hear my side. My ex's side was so well rehearsed, planned and crafted that it made my side seem inconsequential. Everyone in our social circle, friends and family alike, turned a deaf ear to me, and there was absolutely nothing I could do about it.

I will admit, this smear campaign hurt. It hurt a lot. When I attempted to vent to others about it, I was often met with the same response. "Well, if they took his side then they weren't true friends anyway," or "You're better off without those people," or my personal favorite, "You shouldn't let that bother you." But it DID bother me. It perplexed and distressed me and rightfully so. I'll admit that for a time it literally consumed me. Being in a position where you cannot easily defend yourself is a lonely place to be, and that is exactly where I found myself. I wanted so desperately to tell these people what really happened, how I had been traumatized in my marriage, and how my husband was not worthy of their support. The fact was though that I had no outlet to do this.

These “friends” had bought what my husband was selling. He was convincing as a victim, probably giving an Oscar worthy performance to anyone who would listen. I was the bad guy and there was no changing that false narrative. I had to let it, and these “friends” go. And I had to somehow be okay with this.

There was, however, some positivity that was coming from this heart-breaking smear campaign, and I was learning things I never knew, things I never knew I needed to know. I could still be an empathetic person, but I didn’t need to set myself up to be victimized. It was all about understanding the difference. I began developing a thicker skin, and I started to realize that I couldn’t make everyone happy. Not everyone is going to like me and that is perfectly fine. Those individuals that chose to believe my abusive ex-husband had made their decision and cast their loyalty. These people that were blindly supporting this man didn’t need to be part of my life anymore, and I had to let them go and learn to set down what I could no longer carry. I had to shed the bitterness and get on with my plans. Thanks for the memories, but I have a life to fulfill. I once heard a quote that said, “Friends enter our lives for a reason, a season or a lifetime.” These had been seasonal friends and acquaintances, and the seasons were changing.

Tips For Dealing With a Smear Campaign

Stay Calm and Assess the Situation

Don't let your emotions get the best of you.
As maddening as it can be, it is important to look at the facts and document if necessary.

Avoid the Urge To Retaliate

Retaliation can actually make the situation worse.
Know your truth and maintain your dignity.

Seek Out Support

Talk to a therapist or a professional to help you sort out your feelings and emotions.

Protect Your Social Media Accounts

Be careful what you post and don't overshare too much personal information.
Make sure your passwords are up to date.

Focus On You!

As best you can, ignore what others are saying. Shift your focus onto your hobbies and your activities and don't make room for the opinions of others.

Journal Prompt:

What am I holding onto that no longer serves me?

5

CHRISTMAS JEER

"Family is not an important thing. It's everything."

— Michael J. Fox

MY FAMILY IS NOT BROKEN.

It was the month of October when my divorce was finalized, and the holidays were just around the corner. This would be the first holiday season with my disjointed family. My oldest was hundreds of miles away in college, my youngest had finished high school, and I was living as a single person for the first time since my teen years. Thanksgiving came and went quietly without much incident, but the Christmas season felt strange. I found myself thrown back into a pattern of feeling guilty, guilty that my family was no longer together under one roof. It was abundantly clear that my children and I were all happier since the divorce, but I still felt a little melancholy that our holidays would not look as "traditional" as before.

While Christmas had looked like a festive, all-American family holiday in our home for the past twenty plus years, nothing could have been farther from the truth. Up close, our Christmases were exhausting, at least for me. Holidays with a narcissist are anything but joyful. Narcissists want to be the center of attention 365 days out of the year, and when special occasions like birthdays, Mother's Day, and Christmas rear their ugly heads, the narcissist suddenly has competition. Competing with holidays sounds preposterous, but most people who have lived with a narcissist can attest that their behavior gets worse around these special days. My husband was no exception. Christmas is about giving, but in my house giving wasn't about giving from the heart. Instead, it was something to be admired and applauded for. Christmas never felt authentic.

My husband wanted to portray our family as the perfect Norman Rockwell painting, and I will admit that I helped him procure this lie day in and day out. We would begin Christmas Eve with him reading *The Night Before Christmas* by the fireplace. This sounds like a wonderful family tradition, and it should have been. However, nothing with a narcissist is genuine, sadly. It never occurred to me at the time how peculiar it was that he demanded to be videotaped as he read. He wanted a video to prove what a family man he was, or at least thought he was. He wanted it documented that he, the leader of our home, led his family in ringing in the Christmas cheer. The problem was it was all a farce.

Christmas morning had to look perfect, and everyone needed to smile for the pictures. There was one problem leading up to Christmas morning, however. This perceived family man chose not to play a part in any gifting preparations. He didn't really care and couldn't be inconvenienced. I did all of that non-glamorous work. On Christmas Eve, after the kids were nestled in their beds with visions of sugarplums, he would often say, "Show me the list of gifts you got for each of the kids. I need to know what all is wrapped under the tree, so I won't seem surprised when they are opening their presents tomorrow." He needed it to look like he already knew what treasures were inside the beautifully wrapped boxes. After all, he wouldn't want his in-laws to think that he had no part in planning the gifts. He would often request that I choose the most expensive gift under the tree for each of the kids and then sign the gift tag from him. Here kids, look what dad picked out for you! Sadly, I complied year after year. The best gifts never come from Santa. Instead, they came from dad. Dad wanted all the credit. It seems that narcissists even view Santa as a threat.

More than once my husband would request that I purchase my own gifts and wrap them up. He really didn't want to be burdened by shopping. In all fairness I did receive some Christmas gifts over the years, but mostly we agreed to not purchase gifts for each other. However, when we did, I would sometimes be asked to buy my own and place them under the tree with his name as the sender. At the time I didn't think much of it. Go along to get along, that was my mantra. Today I think back to those antics and shake my head. Holidays with narcissists are not holidays at all. They are fake displays of traditionalism, at least they were in my family.

While that first post-divorce holiday season came with a swirl of complicated feelings, I couldn't help but feel a deep sadness at the realization that Christmas would look different for the first time. I felt like my family had lost our traditions, like our familiar routines had quietly slipped away, and I was unsure of how to move forward. Christmas was coming, though, regardless of how weird it may have felt. There was no pause button for adjustment. That first holiday season would be different and once again I didn't feel "normal," at least not in the way I had grown accustomed to, but I did surprisingly feel lighter and definitely more relaxed. I ultimately began to see that the absence of holiday traditions didn't mean the absence of joy. Even in a divorced family, holidays can still be filled with warmth, meaning and cheer.

Christmases without a narcissist in my life have taken on a new meaning. The season no longer feels fake and manufactured, it feels real. Holidays are quiet now, as we don't have an intense personality directing us all to pose and smile for fake family photos. We feel free to just enjoy family time and develop new family traditions.

On that first Christmas after my divorce I felt like my family was a bit disjointed. Today I realize that we are just differently jointed, and different can be good. We are not broken. Instead, we have been reshaped and reassembled with honesty and awareness. We are real. We now can celebrate the season and ring in the New Year with so much more authentic joy, and that's just how it should be. New traditions have room to grow in the space left behind. Christmas in my home feels merry again, and I wouldn't have it any other way.

The Flags I Failed to See

A fast-moving relationship
Feeling "chosen" before feeling known
Being told I am "too sensitive."
Being seen as selfish for needing rest
Apologizing in order to end a circular conversation
Apologizing constantly- sometimes for nothing
Silence used as punishment
Editing myself before speaking
A sense of anxiety when my partner is around
Feeling more at ease when my partner isn't around
Tiptoeing on eggshells
Afraid to bring concerns to my partner
Being repeatedly told I misinterpreted the situation
Sheer confusion after basic interactions with my partner
Constantly wondering what I did wrong
Criticism disguised as honesty
A general lack of empathy in my partner
Stalking framed as care
Compliance being rewarded with peace
Standards that shifted- goalposts constantly being moved
Never feeling like I was enough
Feeling safest when I was alone
Feeling unable to trust myself
I see the color now. The flags were red.

6

A QUIET SPACE

"The deepest loneliness is not being alone, but being with people who make you feel alone."

— Robin Williams

SELF-ISOLATION IS NOT HEALTHY.

In the months following my divorce life began to change. My social circle, or lack thereof, had changed as well. I found that I wasn't interacting with others nearly as much. I was now living in my own place, alone for the first time ever. Life felt exciting and strange at the same time. I was feeling healthier and more alive and experiencing much less anxiety, but while I was thriving, I was also isolating. I would let a few days go by before realizing I hadn't left the house, and I felt okay with this. I was engaging in my hobbies, getting a lot of rest and probably watching too much TV, things that seemed like such a luxury when I was trapped in a toxic marriage. However, I could see a pattern developing and I quickly realized that I needed to break this cycle. Taking time for yourself is good, but not when you completely shut out the world around you, and that is exactly where I was heading.

Some of my desire to isolate and not engage socially came from a place of embarrassment and shame. I dreaded running into people I knew. They would inevitably ask me how I was, and I would feel obligated to say, "Divorced." I felt burdened by the stigma of that word. It felt heavy and loaded with judgement. People would want to know what happened, that is, people who hadn't already heard my ex-husband's version of the story. They would be curious and think, *I thought she was on top of the world?* It seemed too daunting to explain that I had actually been in a toxic marriage, that I was the victim, and now a survivor, of domestic abuse. The disconnect between who they believed I was and the reality was overwhelming. Who in the world would even believe me? The potential of being doubted was more than I wanted to deal with.

Throughout our marriage, my husband donned a false persona in public. My husband, the covert narcissist, looked charming, generous, empathic and caring to the outside world. Never mind that at home he was an abusive manipulator who demanded everyone in the house serve him. He wasn't the only one who was guilty of portraying a lie, however. I was guilty too. It had been my job, or so I thought, to protect his image, protect his ego, and make everyone think he was the wonderful human he pretended to be. Suffice it to say, I was his PR manager for nearly three decades, and I unfortunately did a very good job. Keep up appearances and don't ever let his mask slip- this is how I rolled. This now put me in a tough spot and an embarrassing one, as well. I made it hard for anyone to believe I had actually been a victim, and this very thought kept me from wanting to face others. Everyone would think I had divorced a nice guy and this thought deflated me.

During my marriage, life could be compared to a house in a well-known children's book, The Napping House by Don and Audrey Wood. The story opens with the line, "There is a house, a napping house, where everyone is sleeping." Inside this house a stack of characters are napping in a big, cozy bed. A granny, a child, a dog, a cat and a mouse are all nesting on top of one another on a quiet afternoon. Similar to my marriage, everything seems quiet and appears peaceful. Yet beneath that calm illusion, the structure is precarious. My family, much like this scene, existed in a state of quiet instability. Midway through this story there is an interruption to this fragile peace- a wakeful flea.

The flea bites the mouse,
…which scares the cat,
…which claws the dog,
…which thumps the child,
…who bumps the granny.

This results in the bed breaking and everyone waking. And the flea? That would be me at the point which I decided to exit this marriage. The flea represents the truth. The bed breaks and the carefully maintained secret is exposed. The illusion of peace collapses. The flea wasn't the problem. The flea was the catalyst. That flea was the wake-up call. This call forced everyone to open their eyes, and now no one is napping at The Napping House. While I was glad the secret was out, the hard truth was that I now had to admit my life hadn't been perfect. The jig was up, and it became embarrassing to face friends and acquaintances.

As survivors of trauma, it is also common to be hyper-vigilant to any perceived danger, and the outside world can be a scary place for someone who is recovering from narcissistic abuse. My husband made the world seem terrifying to me throughout our marriage. Narcissists can be notorious for instilling fear in their victims- fear of life itself. My husband leaned a bit into paranoia. He trusted no one and assumed everyone had an angle. As I watched his attitude over the years, a little of that paranoia rubbed off on me. I couldn't help but be completely absorbed by it, as his apprehensions about the world permeated our marriage. Now, living alone for the first time, I found myself frightened of everyone around me. Perhaps this is how my husband wanted me to be, scared of my own shadow. His fear inducing tactics had been successful and for a time I thought that isolating from the world was my safest option, and safety was what I craved.

Another facet of my impending isolation was the fact that I didn't feel "normal." While it certainly wasn't the case, I felt like the only single person on the planet. Mind you, I relished in the act of being single and free, but I feared that somehow people would look at me differently. I was out alone, shopping alone, eating alone, walking through the park alone. I felt like an enigma, like a square peg in a round hole. During my marriage it never bothered me to do these activities alone, but for some reason my thought process shifted now that I was actually a single being. Admittedly, for a time, it seemed safer to stay indoors and keep to myself. I never imagined there would come a time in my life when facing people would become such a challenge, but that is exactly where I had landed.

While I was communicating with others, primarily talking on the phone to my kids and my parents, I was inside my house, Door Dashing my meals and as content as could be. I was fortunate to have the insight to realize that what I was doing, however, was unhealthy. I was in a rut. I was growing too comfortable with the idea of isolation, and I needed to make a change, albeit a gradual one. I could feel a hint of depression creeping in, and I knew this feeling would continue to fester if I didn't do something to stop it in its tracks.

I developed a plan, and it was a simple one. I committed to leaving the house once per day. Some days I went to the grocery store and some days I made my way through a drive-thru for a drink. Other days my outing might be to the local Starbucks for a latte, or maybe just a short walk. In these outings I often didn't talk to many people. However, I was out amongst people, engaging in low-effort social activities, and this helped me to begin to see that I was more "normal" than I thought. No one was staring at me. In fact, no one was paying any attention to the fact that I was moving through my day alone. No one cared. I wasn't sticking out like a sore thumb. I was blending in. I still dreaded the idea of bumping into people I might know, but I was seeing for myself that not every person in the world was bad, and my anxiety and fear of the world began to abate. I became just another person out running errands and living life, and it felt mostly normal and safe and extremely freeing.

About a year into my newfound world of being single, I actually began to see solo outings and activities as a privilege and not a burden. I started to see that I could go where I wanted and do what I wanted without involving anyone else. I didn't need anyone's approval or opinions on my plans. I started to find the joy in only having to answer to myself. The small simple things brought me the most pleasure.

I love to go to the movies, and when I go, I like to arrive early. Really early. Like *way* early. I don't want to take the chance of missing any of the previews. My ex-husband hated this and during our marriage I had to listen to him grumble every time we went to the theatre. He would reiterate time and time again how ridiculous my timetable was, and how unnecessary movie previews were. My small joys were always met with some sort of critique. Now, I don't have to hear it. I can show up as early as I want and no one says a word. It's not so much about catching the previews. It's more about reclaiming my control, a tiny act of self-care that feels surprisingly satisfying.

I have reframed my thinking about solo outings. I used to say things to myself like, "I have to go to the movies alone." Today I say, "I GET to go to the movies alone." I see it as not as a burden or a misfortune, but instead as an entitlement. I get to do things for myself. I get to make my own decisions. These little, seemingly inconsequential things are what I relish most today. I feel much less of a need to isolate now, and while I still have moments of insecurity, I am generally feeling more confident and surer of myself. I'm making my own plans, forging my own path, and living life on my own terms.

Journal Prompt:

What is a small step that you can take to reconnect with the outside world if you are feeling isolated?

7

THE OPEN ROAD

"I am not afraid of storms, for I am learning how to sail my ship." — Louisa May Alcott

---

I AM MORE CAPABLE THAN I IMAGINED.

A couple of years after marrying my husband his job relocated us to one of the largest cities in America. I had grown up in a small town and attended college in a medium sized city, but the big city, and big city traffic, was a new world for me. My rural high school offered drivers ed in the summers and the biology teacher was the instructor. I had a decent education in the rules of the road, and I was a very confident driver in my small town. I later became a somewhat confident driver in larger more congested settings, and I thought I was ready for the next level when I arrived in a major metropolis. The multi-layered, sprawling freeway system most definitely intimidated me, but I was ready and eager to learn.

I wanted to ease into a learning curve and decided that weekend driving would be the safest bet for me. My husband

and I lived in the suburbs, about 40 minutes from the city center, but we would often drive in on the weekends to visit his parents. After several trips into the city and a lot of careful observation, I suggested to my husband that I should drive us on an early Saturday morning. This idea didn't excite him. "No, there is too much traffic today. Maybe next time." Over the course of a few months, I asked, assuming that surely on one of these Saturdays or Sundays the traffic wouldn't be such an issue in his mind. Each time he declined, and each time I attributed his rejection to a protective nature. He's afraid to put me on the freeway system because he is worried about me. He loves me so much he doesn't want me to get hurt.

It didn't take long for me to decide that I couldn't drive the freeways. My husband had told me I couldn't. I wasn't sure why I couldn't, but he must be right. That seed was planted, and it took root. For the next 25 years I wasn't capable of driving outside the small bubble of my suburban community, or so I told myself. Oftentimes my husband would act inconvenienced by my lack of ability. Everyone who knew me knew I didn't drive the freeways; that I couldn't drive the freeways. It became somewhat crippling, but I ultimately always found a way to get where I needed to go, often going way off of the direct route in order to take obscure back roads.

Most of the time, though, I just stayed in my safe space, rarely wandering into the city alone. My husband preferred it this way, not out of love and a sense of protection, but out of a desire for control. It would take me years to recognize the difference. It seemed there was a fine line between love and control in my world, but I always gave my husband the benefit of the doubt. He's not controlling, he just loves me so much. I told myself this lie year after year.

After my divorce at the age of 50, the need arose for me to travel from my southern state to the Midwest to help my parents move after they had sold their home. Logistics made it difficult for anyone to ride with me or drive me on this 10-hour trip, so I got a bold idea. Fresh out of a marriage with freedom ringing in my ears, I decided that I should get in my car and make this trip by myself. I pondered it for weeks, wondering if I was making a mistake. Part of learning to live in freedom was making my own decisions, something I still struggled with greatly.

I wavered back and forth. Some days I felt confident and other days I felt like this drive would be an impossible task. I spoke with a friend about my dilemma. Should I, or shouldn't I? I don't think I can. In fact, I think I need to forget this whole thing. This is a ridiculous idea! Then my friend spoke a sentence to me that completely changed my focus. "You've worked too hard for your autonomy to give up now." I'll admit it- I had to look up the word autonomy on my phone. When I read the definition, I smiled. It means independence and freedom. Yes, there was so much truth to these words, and I knew then that I had to press forward with my plans.

I decided to test the waters by making "practice runs." Two weeks before I was due to leave, I woke up at the crack of dawn on a Sunday morning. I figured the traffic would be minimal and this would be a good time to practice merging onto the freeway. With very sweaty palms I inched my way onto the on ramp and headed north for a 30-minute test drive. I merged on and off a couple of times before making my way back home. Still trembling a bit as I pulled into my garage, I felt accomplished. Maybe this trip wasn't such a crazy idea after all. I would repeat the same routine the following Sunday. This time I drove a little further, all the way to a Cracker Barrel where I treated myself to a delicious breakfast before returning home. The next Sunday would be go time. These 30-50 minute jaunts didn't require nearly the stamina that the 10-hour journey would, but it was a start. I felt somewhat confident and also a little bit excited. To be able to get in my car and drive wherever I wanted had not been a luxury I had been afforded in my marriage. Now, things were changing.

I had worked too hard for my autonomy, and I wasn't going to give up now. I had to repeat this sentence to myself multiple times as I set out for my first ever solo road trip. My car was packed to the hilt, and my 70-pound dog occupied a prominent space in the backseat. There was no turning back now. We were heading to the Midwest, and I was going to get us there.

My practice runs had paid off, and I felt pretty comfortable on the highways, albeit there was more traffic in some areas than I would have liked. With each mile my anxiety loosened, and my confidence rose. I passed the time listening to an audiobook and enjoying several Spotify playlists that I had created especially for the trip. The day was long, very long, but the weather was nice, and everything had fallen into place. It seemed that the universe had decided to be on my side. It was a learning experience, no doubt about it, and I made the trip without incident. Each mile had felt like a small victory.

When I finally pulled into my parents' driveway around 5:00 PM that evening, I felt exhausted and accomplished, but most of all I felt capable. It was a quiet confidence. I brushed it off like it was nothing more than a normal road trip. After all, people drive alone every day. This hadn't been heroic or extraordinary, but in my mind this drive had opened up so many new possibilities. Every decision along this trip had been mine and mine alone, and I had handled it all. I had figured it out. I had gone the distance. Just me, my autonomy and the dog. And I had arrived.

Journal Prompt:

What was your biggest win today?

8

ME, MYSELF AND WHY

"The best minds in mental health aren't the docs.

They're the trauma survivors who have had to figure out how to stay alive for years with virtually no help.

Wanna learn how to psychologically survive under unfathomable stress? Talk to abuse survivors."

— Dr. Glenn Patrick Doyle

SELF-CARE IS NOT SELFISH.

Throughout my marriage self-care had been a luxury. I was expected to be a wife first, then a mother with what time and energy I had left, and finally I could take care of myself. The problem was that there was no time left for me. Sure, I engaged in some free time and did some enjoyable activities, but I was always at the mercy of a narcissist. I often relished in the act of shopping alone or having a lunch date with just myself during the week while my husband was working, and my kids were in school. Acts like this would be talked about by my husband profusely, however. "You sure are lucky that you get to do these fun things while I go to work to support the family," my husband would commonly say. Anything that I did for me was seen as an extreme luxury, something that I should be indebted to my husband for, and oftentimes something that I should feel guilty about doing.

Rest was a source of contention throughout my marriage. My husband saw needing rest as a source of weakness. He saw rest as a personal failure rather than a basic human need. He never failed to make me feel guilty about taking a nap or sleeping too long. If he didn't need rest then no one did, or so he thought. Thus, my sleep schedule had to basically mirror his in order to reduce conflict in our house. I sacrificed rest and felt perpetually exhausted all in the name of trying to deter a meltdown from my husband.

Upon leaving my marriage I struggled with feelings of guilt surrounding any form of self-care. Treating myself to a nice meal or buying something for myself felt absolutely wrong, and when I did something of this nature I questioned if it was okay. I even questioned whether I should take a nap when I was tired, and if I did, I felt a bit guilty. It sounds crazy, but it was ingrained in me to feel as though I deserved none of these "luxuries." Guilt permeated my life in the months after leaving my husband. It almost felt like a luxury to leave, but a luxury that I didn't deserve.

I discussed this guilt that was consuming me with the therapist that I was seeing on a weekly basis. She devised an activity for me. She asked me to write down a list of every traumatic event that I could recall that had happened in my 29 years of marriage. "When you start feeling guilty, I want you to take this list out and read it and remember why you left," she had told me. This ended up being one of the best things that I did in those early days of my departure, and it was a form of self-care that I didn't know I needed. When I read and re-read this list of about 30 or so events it solidified the fact that I needed to leave in order to survive. It gave me the validation of knowing I had made the right choice. This list would also ultimately become the outline for my debut book, *Bride-Made*.

While my marriage had seen some good days and even some good seasons, just one of these bullet points of trauma had been too much on its own. For too long, I had framed my marriage in terms of a math equation. One good day cancels out a bad day, and periods of happiness somehow neutralized times of harm. My reasoning on this subject was simply flawed. Fortunately, this list in my journal made me see things differently. Trauma is trauma, and it doesn't disappear through averaging. Trauma isn't a math equation, and the numbers simply don't matter More importantly, I began to see that my leaving had been the ultimate act of self-care. I was caring for my well-being and my very existence.

The truth is, self-care is not luxurious. It is not asking too much. It is actually necessary for our health. In fact, if you don't take care of yourself then you cannot effectively take care of others. It can be compared to the spiel we get on airplanes. You have to put on our own oxygen mask first before you can help someone else with theirs. Self-care was one of the biggest learning curves for me after my divorce. I had to admit that I definitely felt better, more alive and healthier when I focused on me and my wants and needs.

I began letting myself get more sleep, something I had been so deprived of in the final months of my marriage. I found joy in my hobbies and feeling productive felt amazing. I was in charge of my own home, my own space, and I did with it what I wanted. For the first time in what felt like forever, I enjoyed a peaceful home. It was quiet with no tension in the air, and while I still at times dealt with feelings of anger and hurt, I was truly healing.

In time, self-care became second nature. I didn't have to think about it. I rested when I needed to rest. I learned to pay attention to my body and know my triggers that could lead to anxiety. I started focusing on people who were worthy of my time, not those who had agendas or angles. I found immense joy in my hobbies, and the freedom to dictate my own schedule.

With the guilt cast aside I began to focus on me and found a better version of myself. I was more patient, less on edge, more understanding, more relaxed, and much more joyful. Self-care didn't make the stress in my life mysteriously vanish, but being in a healthier place definitely made it easier for me to deal with stress or difficulties with much more ease. Ultimately, self-care began to feel like a necessity instead of a luxury, like it once had. With a steadier energy I began to feel more like me and that feeling was the true luxury.

SELF-CARE IDEAS

PHYSICAL

Take a walk in nature…Eat healthy…Get a massage…
Be intentional about getting good sleep

EMOTIONAL

Start journaling…Create a vision board…
Listen to music…Pray

SOCIAL

Call a good friend…Practice a random act of kindness…
Spend time with loved ones

SPATIAL

De-clutter and clean…use aromatherapy…
Redecorate or refresh your space

Journal Prompt:

What is one way I can nurture myself this week?

9

A LINE IN THE SAND

"Daring to set boundaries is about having the courage to love ourselves, even when we risk disappointing others." — Brené Brown

---

BOUNDARIES ARE NECESSARY.

Throughout my time in therapy the words "co-dependent" and "boundary" seemed to dominate so many discussions. Apparently, I had too much co-dependency and not enough boundaries. In fact, it seemed I had non-existent boundaries. I knew what boundaries were, as that was obvious to me. I didn't fully grasp the concept of co-dependency. The dictionary defines these two words as:

Boundary - *A limit that separates acceptable behavior from unacceptable behavior.*

Co-dependency - *Psychologically, a state of mutual dependence between two people, especially when one partner relies emotionally on supporting and caring for the other partner.*

As a supposed co-dependent person, I had been living in this dysfunctional dynamic where I was clearly the "giver", and my ex-husband had been the "taker." As a co-dependent, I sacrificed my own well-being and happiness to keep my husband happy and to ward off any meltdowns and outbursts that always lay just around the corner. If he was happy then I was happy. At least that was my definition of happiness during my marriage. Was I actually happy and full of joy? Absolutely not. But happiness and contentedness relied solely on his mood and demeanor, and I was willing to eradicate all of my boundaries to make him happy. Therefore, I guess I fit the definition of a co-dependent person with no boundaries. In a nutshell, I was the perfect partner for a narcissist. I had been moving through life with a target on my back and I didn't even know it.

Throughout all of my reading and research on these terms, co-dependency and boundaries, and their core meanings within the field of psychology, it occurred to me that both of these issues are rooted in one larger issue, people pleasing. I was definitely a people pleaser, and always had been (and probably always will be.) Had people-pleasing been the culprit which led me right into this marriage with a narcissist? After some careful reflecting I can now say yes, I believe it was.

On the surface, I do not believe being a people-pleaser is necessarily a bad thing. My desire to please is not the result of any trauma or negativity in my life. It is simply part of my personality as an empath. For as long as I can remember I have been highly in-tune to the emotions of others. It is basically a heightened sensitivity. I am very intuitive, and I love to help others. These aren't bad qualities, but empaths who don't build strong boundaries can certainly become targets for people like narcissists.

There is a fine line between a "good" kind of people pleasing and a "bad" kind of people pleasing, and that is one thing I failed to understand in the early years of my marriage. If you are catering to someone because you truly want to and you are expecting nothing in return, then that type of people pleasing is pure and genuine and healthy. However, if you are catering to someone in order to elicit a certain emotion, or in my case warding off negative emotions, then that type of people pleasing is not healthy. That is where boundaries are broken, and co-dependency takes up residence. This is where I had built my home of internal dysfunction.

About two years after the birth of my oldest child I developed a case of shingles. I had never experienced this condition before and I was surprised to learn that it could be triggered by stress, which I had in ample supply. I was also surprised at how these small red spots on my torso could cause so much discomfort. While I caught it early and only had a few spots to contend with, I was miserable and the medication that I was put on made me feel even worse. It certainly wasn't a serious case of shingles at all, but I was most definitely under the weather and trying to keep up with a lively two-year-old all at the same time.

A couple of days after I was diagnosed, and still feeling very poorly, my husband decided that we should all go and visit his parents, who lived about an hour away. He arranged for us to go to his parents' home and then out to a restaurant for lunch. It would be a fun-filled family day. While this sounded somewhat pleasant, I knew I didn't feel up to going. This would have been a good time to enact a boundary, and it should have sounded like this:

"I don't feel like going today. I need to stay home and take it easy. You can go on by yourself."

Instead, my people-pleasing, co-dependent self with no boundaries said:

"Okay, I'll get myself ready and pack the baby's things and we can leave whenever you're ready."

Was I agreeing to do something I didn't feel like doing for the purpose of showing kindness to my husband? No. I was appeasing his whims and wishes so I didn't have to deal with the fallout. If I had refused to go, he would have been angry. There would have been conflict. He may have pouted and given me the silent treatment for days, or he may have become verbally abusive, telling me that I always ruin his plans, that I'm not fun enough or that he is tired of dealing with my issues. I didn't want to face this conflict. In my mind it was the lesser of two evils to just go and please him. And that's, ashamedly, what I did. Against my better judgement, I went along to get along.

I have since learned that the ability to say no is a learned skill. Creating boundaries can also create conflict, and that is not necessarily a bad thing. Conflict brings issues to the forefront instead of sweeping them under the rug, and maybe conflict is what I needed in the early days of my marriage. Through conflict I might have gained a better understanding of who I was married to, and my marriage may have dissolved more quickly. Instead, I stayed. I people pleased, I appeased, and I sacrificed myself for nearly three decades.

Education would have been my way out long ago. Instead, it took me far too long to fully embrace the meanings of co-dependency and boundaries and understand that people pleasing can invite toxic behaviors and toxic people into our lives. There is nothing wrong with kind acts, a kind heart and a desire to help and please others. The issue can lie in offering these things without limits. Learning where to draw the line is essential. Boundaries do not diminish kindness. Instead, boundaries protect our own peace.

Journal Prompt:

What does a healthy boundary look like to me?

10

ABSOLUTE VALUES

"Black and white thinking: simple, safe and spectacularly wrong" — Unknown

---

SMALL MISTAKES ARE NOT THE END OF THE WORLD.

My world was black and white for 29 years. There was no grey, no middle ground. We lived in extremes. All good or all bad, fantastic or despicable, highs, lows and absolutely nothing in between. Dichotomous thinking. Unfortunately for their victims, this cognitive distortion is a very common thinking and reasoning pattern for a narcissist. In most cases it is probably just another one of their defense mechanisms, designed to protect their fragile yet narcissist egos. They may initially see their partner or spouse as perfect and unblemished. However, one small mistake or flaw can have their partner descending into a black hole of failure with no chance of escape.

During our marriage my husband saw not a hint of grey, ever. The smallest mistake, in his mind, meant the end of the world or utter catastrophe. His extreme reactions to small flaws should have been a red flag to me, but I wasn't well versed in seeing flags. Instead, I initially saw a personality quirk. These quirks seemed like harmless eccentricities that I could eventually adapt to. Later, he had me convinced that his catastrophic thinking and his way of anticipating disaster actually made our lives easier and kept us from running into problems. I began to think he was right. He often reminded me that he was the smartest man in the room and that he knew more than anyone. Therefore, his crazy manner of doing things must be the right way, or so I thought. His distorted view of reality ultimately shaped mine, and his absurdness became my normal.

When trying to conceive our first child, my husband and I ran into fertility issues. I routinely purchased ovulation predictor kits, but I also used a more basic method of prediction as recommended by my fertility specialist, temperature monitoring. I would take my temperature each morning, waiting for that spike that would indicate I was ovulating. The most accurate way to do this, at the time, wasn't with the digital thermometers, but instead with the very basic mercury thermometers. If you're old enough to remember these antique relics, you know that you had to shake them vigorously to set the red line to zero before placement under your tongue. Well, on one particular day as I was shaking this small piece of elongated glass, I accidentally hit it on the dresser causing the thermometer to break and fall onto the carpeted floor in my bedroom. This doesn't sound like it should be the catastrophic end of the world, but think again. I lived with a narcissist.

My husband was mortified that I could be so careless. Apparently, he had never broken anything in his entire life, at least that's how he acted. In my house there were no such things as small mistakes. All or nothing, black or white, perfect or utter devastation. My husband immediately began listing all of the problems this broken thermometer would cause in our lives. His lecturing went on for several days. I was constantly reminded how careless I had been, how dangerous mercury was and how it was now in our carpet. This conversation escalated to ridiculous proportions and ultimately my husband decided we would never be able to sell our house if one day we decided to move. Huh? I had no idea what to do with this information. I was literally sick with worry. Had I really destroyed our house and created an environmental crisis? I was just waiting for the EPA to show up at my front door. That's sure how dire my husband had made this sound. I couldn't be the only person who had ever broken a thermometer, surely? Apparently, I was, and it was now the end of the world. His absolute thinking convinced me of this.

Over the course of the next couple of weeks my husband finally let the issue go. While he would refer to my mistake periodically over the course of our marriage, his abhorrent lecturing on the matter finally ceased. Despite his dire predictions, the world did not stop spinning. There was no intervention by the Environmental Protection Agency. No lives were lost. And I should also mention that two years later we did in fact sell that house. Mercury and all.

Today, I have to constantly remind myself that small mistakes aren't going to end the world. It's okay to exist in shades of grey. Life doesn't have to be "all or nothing." Some things fall in between good and utter catastrophe. Some things can just be okay, and that in itself is perfectly okay. Life with absolutes is incredibly exhausting. Swinging from one extreme to the other leaves no room to breathe. I am learning, slowly and deliberately, to relax and let some things go. Mistakes will happen; they always do. But the sun will most assuredly still rise, and tomorrow will offer a new change to begin again. Today I am intentionally choosing grace over panic, and I am reclaiming a steadier and more peaceful way of living.

Journal Prompt:

What are three shades of grey that can exist between success and failure?

11

BREATHING ROOM

"Society has obviously been worshipping the wrong heroes this whole time because I'm convinced it takes less strength to pick up a building than it does to permanently leave an abusive situation." — Colleen Hoover, It Starts with Us

---

FREEDOM IS PRICELESS.

Early in my marriage I experienced a loss of freedom and a loss of control. The problem was, I didn't even realize it was happening. It had been a slippery slope. Narcissistic personality disorder tends to get worse with age and my husband's control seemed to tighten like a vice with each passing year. My time became his time, and my possessions were his possessions. I was in my 40's and at the end of my rope when it became obvious to me that every minute of my day was being scrutinized, criticized and controlled. I longed for freedom. I craved time to myself and found more peace sitting in my car alone than being inside my own home.

I was always looking for some sort of mental escape during those years to help me cope with the misery that seemed to engulf me. I ultimately landed a side job that was online. It was a measly payout, but it was certainly a fun distraction from my everyday life. The job involved captioning TV shows and movies for an online company. I quickly worked my way up to a "pro" level, and as a result, I got my pick of some of the better projects. In order to maintain this standing, I had to caption a set number of minutes per month, so I ended up "working" a couple of hours a day, trying to keep up a consistent schedule. The beauty of this job was that I could work anytime and anywhere. Oftentimes, I worked at night when the house was quiet. Sometimes I snuck away during the day and distracted myself with a little TV and typing. However, no matter when or where I worked, it infuriated my husband.

My husband saw this side job as a waste of time. This was time that I should be spending with him. In his mind there was no need for me to work. He was the ultimate provider, and I wanted for nothing, except peace of mind. He didn't understand that I wasn't working for the slim salary. I was working to protect my sanity. Nonetheless, he decided that I shouldn't be allowed to continue with this nonsense, and he ultimately did something about it. He picked up my laptop computer, right in front of me, and proceeded to carry it into another room. I didn't follow him, as I wasn't sure what he was doing. I soon discovered, however, that he had hidden my computer. This was his solution to my "time management problem." At least that's how he saw it.

My computer remained hidden for two weeks, and I said nothing about it. I pretended not to notice in an effort to minimize conflict. Instead, and in order to maintain my captioning status, I pulled out an old laptop. This was one that my husband had fortunately forgotten about. I continued on with my work out of his sight, and then one day my computer magically returned. I walked into my bedroom one afternoon and it was sitting on top of my husband's dresser. I asked him, "Where has my computer been for the last two weeks?" His response was unbelievable. "I don't know. I'm pretty sure it's been on the dresser all this time." I shook my head. How could he make that statement with such calm certainty? He was the ultimate gaslighter, the kind of person who could twist and reshape reality into anything he wanted it to be. As he stood there with his smug expression, he really thought I would believe this ridiculous claim. There was no gain in trying to argue with him. A confrontation would only lead to circular conversations, and I was in no mood to deal with that. So, I picked up my computer and proceeded to continue on with my day.

After my divorce, the level of freedom that I experienced was almost overwhelming. Suddenly, I could do what I wanted, when I wanted. I could wake up each morning and decide how I wanted to spend my day, and I didn't need anyone's approval or permission. My belongings belonged to ME, and no one could hide my things in an effort to control me. The idea of this freedom was fun, exciting and quite honestly terrifying. It was such a diversion to what I had lived for nearly three decades, and I wasn't entirely sure what to do with myself. It was a bit like being in a lake when I was only used to a bathtub. I had been so confined in that tub with porcelain walls all around me. Venturing into the lake was amazing. There was room to move, room to float, room to exhale. However, it also left me unsure of what to do with myself. My environment was suddenly so vast, and I wasn't sure what direction I should take.

I feared I didn't have the capability to run my household and to make necessary decisions. After all, my husband had ingrained in me that I didn't have the necessary skills to manage. I wasn't smart enough or knowledgeable enough about anything to be successful in keeping my life together, according to him. I doubted myself in the beginning and it certainly took some time for me to realize that I could do this. I could manage my day-to-day life, my finances, my time and my home, and I could do it very well. Every day was a learning experience, sometimes frustrating and sometimes wonderful.

Many victims of narcissists are led to believe that they aren't capable and don't have the life skills or intelligence to run their lives and their households. However, most of these victims have probably been running more of their day to day lives that they realize. Male narcissists don't make the best fathers, and oftentimes the female victim feels like a single parent, managing the day-to-day life of the kids. Narcissistic fathers tend to show up when it looks good or when it's fun, not when it's necessary. Victims living with a narcissistic partner likely manage all of the not-so-fun aspects of their homes, like taking care of the house and all of the mundane things that keep a family running. Even though most victims are told they aren't capable, they are likely more capable than they realize, and this was what I experienced. As a survivor of narcissistic abuse, I had already lived through a juggling act of complete dysfunction. I could certainly handle a life that was calm and ordered.

I found, in the early days of my single hood, that I had a great need to control my space. I needed complete organization. For some reason this calmed me. If anything was in disarray, I found myself beginning to panic. I could quite literally feel physical symptoms when faced with disorganization or chaos of any kind. I believe this was due to an overwhelming need to have control, something I had been deprived of for so long. I was considerate of myself and realized this quirk would become a way of life for me. Organization is not a bad thing after all! However, I did have to learn, in time, that moments of disorganization were not the end of the world. Messes are okay, and my house doesn't have to be perfect every single day. It would take time for me to relax my compulsions, but at least I understood the reasons for feeling the way that I did. In time, my need for control would lessen as I began to feel less threatened and more confident.

Freedom after abuse was a big concept to wrap my head around. I had gone from complete control to complete freedom quite literally overnight. It does take time to sort it all out and to find the confidence to make decisions, but after a period of healing I can say that my freedom is something I will never take for granted again. I try to be intentional about being grateful every day for my freedom to live how I choose, and there is no price tag you can place on that level of peace.

Journal Prompt:

Think of a moment when you felt truly independent. What was that experience like for you?

12

ABOVE THE CLOUDS

Do one thing every day that scares you." — *Eleanor Roosevelt*

I CAN FACE MY BIGGEST FEARS.

For as long as I can remember I have been afraid of flying. My first flight was as a middle schooler and the destination was Disney World. The initial take-off in a small prop plane terrified me, and the sensation of rising off the ground was almost more than I could take. However, I acclimated to the plane, and the subsequent legs of the trip were not nearly as bad. I returned from the happiest place on Earth in one piece with good memories, but not exactly anxious to fly again.

The next time I would board a plane would be in college, and this time I was with my future husband. We were traveling to his hometown to visit his family during the Christmas season. He was also a somewhat nervous flyer and would often remind me that my fear actually fueled his fear. We took a handful of flights together during our college years and each one was a little worse than the previous. Our mutual fears fed off of one another and we made the very worst travel companions.

During my senior year in college my soon to be husband and I took a very memorable flight to a family member's wedding. It was memorable, but not in a good way. My fiancé decided that the easiest way to deal with my phobia would be for me to drink before the flight. He assumed that I would be less trouble for him if I was intoxicated, I presume. He was the seasoned flier, and I thought he knew more than me. Although I was not someone who enjoyed alcohol, I had heard that a drink before a flight really helped to calm one's nerves. This sounded good to me. I figured it might take the edge off, allowing me to feel more relaxed on this flight. Maybe this was in fact the answer for me. It seemed like a quick and easy solution to my crippling phobia.

Arriving at the airport, my fiancé took out a Coke bottle that he had prepared before leaving home. Mixed with the Coke was Jack Daniels. He assured me this would be the best thing for me to drink to prepare me for the flight. Feeling like he was the "smart" one in this relationship, I went with his suggestion. It was the worst tasting concoction I had ever consumed, but he said it would work. And so, I drank. He had measured out just the right amount, or so he told me. I'm not sure what kind of scale he had used, but I spent the entirety of the flight violently ill. Never mind being a nervous flier. I was nervous about the alcohol killing me! My fiancé perhaps unknowingly (or maybe not) had given me way too much, and I was too naive in the alcohol world to even realize it.

I was nauseous for the next two days, and this man never once showed an ounce of concern. We had family festivities to attend to and people to visit with. I wasn't allowed to be sick. To my fiancé, it was all about showing up, looking good and putting on a happy face. Never mind that he had nearly given me alcohol poisoning the day before. There was no time for queasy stomachs. Narcissists can't be inconvenienced by such trivial things, and my fiancé was certainly no exception. Over time, the story of my getting drunk on the plane became a favorite anecdote around friends and family. The flight attendant's words to me as I had exited the plane that evening would later become comic relief at its finest. "I need to inform you that it is technically against FAA regulations for you to be on a plane in your condition."

I later learned to laugh about my experience with Jack Daniels and that infamous flight, deep inside knowing the actual danger that my husband had subjected me to.

I flew a few more times with my husband in the subsequent years, but for the majority of our marriage I kept both feet on the ground. No flying for me. I was finished. Suffice it to say, he had taken my phobia and made it into something debilitating. For many years, I was blamed with being the family travel party pooper. We couldn't go on nice trips because I wouldn't fly. We couldn't be a normal family because I refused to get on a plane. Look how much fun everyone on Facebook seems to be having. Too bad we can't be like that. My husband reminded me often that he was giving up the fun side of life for me. I was a burden, a huge burden. I had a crippling phobia that no other husband would put up with but him, or so he said. No one else would ever want to be married to someone like me, and I should definitely count myself lucky that my husband was agreeable to drive places. This narrative would be a constant in our marriage for nearly three decades.

After my divorce and after my first book had been published, I received an invitation to speak at a women's retreat in Florida. It sounded so exciting, and I couldn't fathom turning down such an honor. The only thing holding me back was the mode of transportation. Due to the distance, I would have no choice but to fly. It had been nearly 20 years since I had last been on a plane. I seriously considered declining this opportunity. I just wasn't sure I could muster the courage to board an airplane and fly the friendly skies, not to mention I would be traveling solo. Then I remembered that "autonomy" discussion before my road trip. It kept playing over and over in my head like a song that just wouldn't leave me alone.

"You've worked too hard for your autonomy to give up now."

I finally agreed that I had worked too hard on myself to stop now. It was true. So, I sat down at my computer one evening, and I booked a single round-trip plane ticket. This time I would be traveling alone. I would be facing my biggest fear, but this time I would be doing it with a new frame of mind. This decision was rooted in choice rather than pressure, and I had a mission to accomplish. My husband had told me for years how I was not "normal" and that my phobias were exaggerated and unfounded. I felt like the square peg in a round hole for much of my marriage. I was constantly trying to make myself fit in a shape that was not meant for me.

Still, a part of me longed to feel "normal." Normal people fly every day without a second thought, so I decided that if I could fly, I too could feel like I fit in with the rest of the world, just as I was. It would be a challenge to myself, perhaps my biggest challenge to date. Booking that airline ticket was like a declaration. I was proving to myself that I could challenge the narrative I had been given and replace it with my own.

The morning of my flight I arrived at the airport before daylight. The weather was perfect, and clear skies were in the forecast. Traveling solo to a destination where I knew not one soul was scary. It was also scary that I was about to board a plane for the first time in so many years. I decided for my own personal safety that I should appear confident. I needed to look like I navigated airports every day, when in fact I had no idea what I was doing. So, I followed the crowd. I carefully watched other people who were in line in front of me, and I mimicked their actions. Sure, I do this all the time. I acted like a seasoned traveler and I pulled it off pretty well, I think. I checked my bag and sailed through the TSA line like a pro, and when it was time to board, I was determined that no one would know I was terrified.

I settled into my first-class seat at the very front of the plane. I had treated myself to this tier simply because I wanted to feel the least amount of sensation as possible when the plane took off. If I could make it through the take off, then the battle would be half won. I put on my noise cancelling headphones (a must for fearful fliers), and I cued up my curated playlist of relaxing music. I looked calm and serene, but I considered more than once the idea of getting off the plane and calling it quits. Each time the urge would take hold, I would concentrate on the music playing through my headphones, and before I knew it the plane was taxiing down the runway. Now it was too late to turn back, and I had a moment of panic, internal panic. I would venture to say I was the most scared person on the flight that morning, but no one knew, I was sure of it. I tuned out the world and before I knew it, we were wheels up on the way to Florida.

The flight was mostly smooth and I'm not sure I opened my eyes even once. In fact, I missed the opportunity to get my small bag of pretzels. At one point, I glanced over and saw the passenger next to me drinking a soda and enjoying this menial snack. The flight attendant must have assumed I was asleep and passed me right by, and I was okay with that. I had been too nervous to have any sort of appetite anyway. I was just glad that the flight was nearing an end and that I could feel the beginnings of a descent.

Upon landing, I would be on my way to a retreat where I would spend the next four days with a group of women I had never met in my life. This was so far out of my comfort zone, but I pushed through. My comfort zone had kept me safe, but this departure from what was familiar would be proof that I was growing and that I was healing. I had just endured a two-hour flight to be here, and me and my autonomy couldn't give up now. I ended up meeting lots of new faces at this retreat, making friends and getting to share my story in front of a group where it was so well received. I left this retreat with so much more confidence than I had arrived with. The flight and the anxiety had actually been worth it. I had pushed my own boundaries, and I had reaped the rewards.

The trip home was uneventful, though my fear was still very much present. The take-off was easier, the flight was bumpier, but all in all it was manageable for me. This time I was able to open my eyes mid-flight and actually enjoy a little bit of the in-flight entertainment. I distracted myself by watching an episode of "Friends," while continually checking the flight map and clock to see how many more minutes I had to remain in the air. When the wheels touched down my imaginary sigh of relief was unforgettable. I had done it. The trip was complete. I had booked a flight, boarded a plane, flown to another state, given a public presentation, and flown home. And I had done it completely by myself. What would my ex-husband think if he knew? Who cares. This wasn't the time to focus on him. As I stepped off the plane and headed toward the baggage terminal, I felt something I hadn't felt in many long years. Normal.

Journal Prompt:

What is your biggest fear and why?

Signs You Are Healing From Narcissistic Abuse

1. You no longer feel a desire to reach out or contact them.

2. You no longer care who they are with or what they are doing.

3. You are living for you and no one else.

4. You are achieving new heights of success.

5. You find it easier to make decisions without questioning yourself.

6. You feel more alive and energized.

7. Your physical health improves.

8. Your confidence returns.

9. You find a new social circle.

10. You no longer face each day with dread, but instead with joy.

13

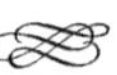

TRIPODS

"Be still and know that I am God." — Psalms 46:10

MY FAITH SUSTAINS ME.

The idea of starting anew after years of emotional and psychological abuse was daunting, but starting over was the only choice I had in order to save myself and my mental health. After moving into my own apartment for about nine months, I found a townhome in the middle of town. My new place was a short walk to Starbucks and various cafes and shopping spots, and it seemed like the perfect dwelling for me to start a new chapter.

As I slowly began the moving process I spent my days sorting through boxes of essentials, of keepsakes and memories, and organizing a new life for myself. During this unpacking phase I kept finding something rather puzzling, tripods. I had never purchased a single one of these tripods. I didn't know where they had come from, as I had never seen any of them before. Box after box revealed random tripods in all different sizes, some larger ones for attaching cameras, and some smaller ones for attaching cellphones. I found tripods in boxes of dishes, boxes of books, even boxes of clothes. I found about five or six in total. At one point, I said out loud to myself, "Why are there so many tripods?" I stacked them all together in a corner of my garage, and the pile grew with each emptied box.

At 49 years old I had successfully moved out of the home I had shared with my husband, but the biggest battle was still ahead, the divorce. I was terrified and anxious. I spent a good deal of time praying about this frightening but very necessary next step. Always one to pray, I can't say I had ever actually heard God's voice speak to me, though I had felt His guidance many times. That all changed in the month leading up to my filing. I began to hear God's voice say to me, "I am sending you three people to carry you through." While I didn't actually hear an audible voice, I heard the idea instead. It kept entering my thought process. Three people. I kept getting a message of "three" over and over again. The number three would pop into my head at random times, or I would notice the number three in varying places. It was perplexing and strange, until one day when it all made sense. The tripods.

When I Googled the word "tripod," the actual definition struck me. A tripod is a portable three-legged frame or stand, used as a platform for supporting the weight and maintaining the stability of some other object. God was providing me with a "tripod" of people. These people would represent the stand, while I would be the one requiring the stability. Three. I was certain about the identities of these people. My mom and dad would be the first two legs, and a close friend would be the third. A tripod cannot stand with just two legs. All three legs must work equally in unison in order to support weight and provide a stable base. These three people, unbeknownst to them, would work in unison to make up the strongest team ever.

Throughout the nearly one-year journey of my divorce, my "tripod" of people saw to my every need. I was completely covered in every way. The first two legs of the tripod, my mom and dad, provided all of the financial support. They made sure I had a good, safe place to live and that I would be in no danger. They helped me financially in those early days when my husband had drained our bank account in an effort to make my life difficult. Their physical presence at every legal meeting was a given. They planned and calculated and advised, making sure I would land in a good place and that I would always feel protected.

The third tripod leg was like the emotional lifeline. My best friend was someone I could talk to incessantly about anything and everything. It was the best therapy money could buy, only it was free. We talked about my abuse and how it had shaped me. We talked about mental health. We talked about faith. We prayed. And through our daily talks, I slowly began to heal. Our talks gave me the opportunity to really process my feelings, and this was invaluable to my self-esteem. My confidence was built up with each passing day, and I was made to feel like I could conquer any obstacle that I faced.

The immense effort that was poured into restoring me was unlike anything I'd ever witnessed. Throughout the ordeal, my Type A personality never required medication. No anti-depressants, no anti-anxiety drugs. I sailed through a massively high conflict divorce with no panic attacks (something I had been plagued with throughout my marriage). And while I did experience anxiety throughout this process, it paled in comparison to what I had experienced in the past. I was calm, I was confident, and I was happy. Seem impossible? Yes, it does, but it happened. God knew what he was doing when he placed those three people in my life.

After my divorce was final, nearly one year later, I was cleaning out a storage unit. I came across a very nice black canvas zippered bag that I had never seen before. Being curious, I carefully unzipped the bag right there in the storage facility and inside I discovered a brand new, previously unopened, still in plastic, gold colored tripod. One last reminder that God had seen me through this divorce just like he said he would. A reminder that he had given me three people, just like he said he would. My tripod of support. I would not have made it through this season of my life and emerged in one piece without all three of these tripod legs. These three legs provided equal support. An equal effort from each person. A rock-solid team that literally saved my life.

God moves in mysterious ways, it's true. Since my divorce more than two years ago, I am still seeing tripods everywhere. It's usually when I least expect it, but when I am needing a reminder of God's presence and his promise. Today when I see a tripod, I take notice and I smile. God provides, protects and comforts, and sometimes He uses the most peculiar analogies in order to get our attention.

14

THERE GOES THE NEIGHBORHOOD

"Light a match, leave the past, burn the ships and don't you look back" — For King and Country, Burn the Ships

---

Two years after my divorce was final, I embarked on the biggest rebuilding part of my healing. A literal rebuilding. I decided to build a house. After many months of thinking and planning and pondering, I decided the healthiest next move for me was a physical move out of the state that I had called home for the past 25 years.

After enduring the smear campaign everything in my town just felt toxic. I was actually feeling more confident, and I was no longer anxious to leave my house. Bumping into people I knew in public, who had probably heard untruths about me, didn't really bother me anymore. The possibility of bumping into my ex in our small community was a manageable concept too. But the simple fact was this, I would rather not. I would rather not put myself in that position. Could I? Of course. Do I want to? Absolutely not. A fresh start to my new life seemed more attainable outside of the community where I had resided for so many years. I made the decision to move out of state and back to my hometown, where I had grown up.

Factoring into my decision to move, although mostly fueled by a desire for a new start, was the fact that my ex-husband and his new wife had decided to rent a townhome across the street from me. Not in the same neighborhood or down the street, but directly across the street. This was intimidation at its best. The neighborhood where I live is truly the perfect location. It's the best spot for people wanting to live amongst all of the wonderful amenities the community has to offer, and I'm sure this factored into my ex's decision to rent a second home there. It can't be overlooked, however, this is also the perfect spot where he could succeed in making me uncomfortable. I'm sure he relished in the idea of keeping tabs on me. It's as though he was trying to say, "I'll always be watching. You'll never be rid of me." To him, this new residence would be more than a home, it would be a statement with cruelty as its motivator.

My ex-husband would also love the fact that as a neighbor, I would have a front row seat to the charade of his new life: His new wife, his extravagant way of living and all of his flashy possessions. In his twisted-up mind this would make me jealous, or at least he would hope it would make me jealous. As a narcissist he is literally convinced that everyone wants everything he has. To think that I would envy a life with him or envy his new wife's status is simply laughable. I had already made my choice two years prior, and I chose peace over chaos and abuse. My parting gifts of health and a newfound confidence held the maximum value. However, in his mind, he would be demonstrating to me just what I had given up when I made the decision to walk away from him. Thanks, but no thanks. Good riddance.

So, I decided to move and to build, both literally and figuratively. To be clear, I wasn't running from my problems with my ex-husband. I had already faced these problems head on. Instead, I was choosing not to put myself in problematic or destabilizing situations. I was choosing not to invite chaos back into my world. I was choosing peace of mind and my safety and my sense of calm. I was choosing a new life, a new house and a fresh start. I was choosing me.

With the construction of my new house, I would be making all of the decisions. I didn't need anyone's approval, and it certainly didn't matter what my ex thought. This was all me, and it was the most freeing thing I had engaged in so far. I would choose the style, the colors and all of the finishings and details. I chose what I liked. Back in my marital years I would have chosen what he liked, to make him happy, to gain his acceptance and to ward off conflict. Go along to get along. I wouldn't have even known what I liked. Furthermore, I wouldn't have trusted my own decisions if I had even been allowed to make them. Today I'm learning what I like and what I want. I chose colors and styles for my house that represented me and no one else. This would be my home and my creation, and not one part of him would be allowed to seep through the cracks.

Watching the building process of this house had so many parallels to the process of rebuilding my identity, the one that had been lost so many years ago in my marriage. Laying the foundation, making sure the ground was even and smooth was like the stripping away of everything I was in that marriage and beginning again. Watching the walls go up was akin to creating boundaries, strong ones at that. Then, seeing all of the detail come together was like rediscovering who I was, what I liked and what I wanted, my desires and my dreams. A new house, a new state, and a new beginning.

While I am still figuring it all out, I think I have a good foundation. Every day, I grow a little more and gain more clarity about who I am. Healing is not a single act. It's like building a house, brick by brick, and being intentional about the choices I make. Healing comes with ups and downs. Parts of me may never heal, and that's okay. My experiences have made me who I am today, and I'm starting to like me. I'm excited for the future ahead and a new chance at a life that can bring me so much peace and happiness.

As I write the words to this last memoir chapter I am sitting at my desk in my new home. I've been here just two weeks now. The boxes are unpacked, and I am slowly settling into the rhythm of this new life. It's peaceful here, and it's the kind of peace I don't take for granted. This peace comes from safety, intention and hard-earned self-trust. I already love this life not because it is perfect, but because it is mine. I can't predict how this next chapter will unfold, but I've made plans.

I'm not going to let intimidation get the best of me. Fear won't be allowed to dictate my actions.

I'm going to have a better understanding of my self-worth. I have set a higher bar, and I will stick to it.

I am going to let go of people and friends who are not meant to occupy space in my life. My time is best spent with those who are worthy of my time.

I'm going to see my family as whole and intact instead of broken, and I am going to look forward to creating new traditions with them.

I am making a point to not self-isolate, and I am focusing on my mental health. I am going to take care of me.

I am realizing I am capable of far more than I ever thought. The sky's the limit!

I am prioritizing self-care and taking better care of my overall health. I am going to focus on doing what's best for my well-being.

I am developing boundaries, and I will do my best to stick to them.

I am okay with mistakes, and I am realizing that I don't have to be perfect. Mistakes aren't the end of the world.

I am learning how to enjoy my newfound freedom, and I will never take that freedom for granted ever again. I will wake up each morning feeling grateful for a new day that I can plan.

I am pushing past my fears to find such an exciting life out there. Fear held me back for too long, but not anymore.

Finally, I am leaning into my faith, knowing that God is with me and will never leave. His presence will guide me wherever I decide to go.

These are my plans, my carefully drawn blueprints for rebuilding a life that is entirely mine. The future is wide open, vibrant and waiting.

Dear Reader,

You've just been given a glimpse into my healing journey, healing from abuse and healing from the aftermath of divorce. If you've found yourself in a similar situation to mine, please know that healing is not linear. There is no deadline for recovery, no finish line, no rulebook. Sometimes healing is quiet, and sometimes it is loud, but as long as there is forward movement, you are heading in the right direction. Be kind to yourself. Give yourself the space and the grace to stumble and room to learn and grow.

Have you considered journaling? The therapeutic benefits that can come from picking up a pen and a notebook are plentiful. Bullet journals are wonderful for making lists and crafting plans. If you've never journaled before, this type of writing or list-making can seem much less daunting. Blank books are a great tool too, giving you wide open spaces to write whatever is on your mind. It's a safe place to talk and speak words that may be too hard to vocalize. Through journaling, you can revisit your pages later down the road and have a first-hand account of your healing, seeing just how far you've come.

Vision boards can be a fun and creative way to make plans and create a blueprint for yourself. Along your healing journey, you will need to gather some new ideas, make changes, and plan for a new way of life. Whether it's a change due to divorce or a change of mindset, vision boards are great for dreaming and discovering who you really want to be. These boards also provide a visual goal so you can actively see what you are working toward. This is a way to dream, plan, organize and chart your progress. You may even discover ideas that you never knew you had.

The end of a marriage or a lifestyle might signify the end to life as you know it, but maybe you never wanted that life you once knew. In my case, that life was one of control and manipulation. It was a carefully constructed cage that kept me from seeing what was possible. I wanted better. I wanted more, and maybe, deep down, you do too. It's never too late to make a change, to save yourself and find a better life outside of the constraints of control or abuse. Tomorrow is a new day. It's a blank page, a wide-open road. Take that first step. Make plans.

— Mia

Vision board

Health	Career goals
Family	Financial
Travels	Hobbies
Relationships	

BRIDE-MADE

This memoir chronicles the author's harrowing journey through a marriage overshadowed by covert narcissistic abuse. Starting from a seemingly perfect courtship filled with grand gestures, the book delves into how these acts masked deeper patterns of control and manipulation. Through raw and vivid storytelling, the author unpacks her three-decade-long experience, highlighting moments of self-doubt, realizations, and eventual awakening to her abusive reality. With each chapter, the layers of a toxic relationship unravel, exposing not only her struggles but also her resilience.

*Bride-Made is a courageous testament to survival and self-discovery. It's not just a story of abuse but a guide for others to recognize and break free from similar patterns. I'd recommend this book to anyone seeking to understand covert narcissism, especially those in toxic relationships who feel unseen or unheard. The raw honesty and relatable an*ecdotes *make it both heartbreaking and empowering."*

-Literary Titan

Diagnostic criteria (DSM-5-TR) for Narcissistic Personality Disorder

- A grandiose sense of self-importance (e.g., the individual exaggerates achievements and talents and expects to be recognized as superior without commensurate achievements)
- A preoccupation with fantasies of unlimited success, power, brilliance, beauty, or ideal love
- A belief that he or she is special and unique and can only be understood by, or should associate with, other special or high-status people or institutions
- A need for excessive admiration
- A sense of entitlement (i.e., unreasonable expectations of especially favorable treatment or automatic compliance with his or her expectations)
- Interpersonally exploitive behavior (i.e., the individual takes advantage of others to achieve his or her own ends)
- A lack of empathy (unwillingness to recognize or identify with the feelings and needs of others)
- Envy of others or a belief that others are envious of him or her
- A demonstration of arrogant and haughty behaviors or attitudes

Glossary of Narcissism

Blame Shifting: A manipulation tactic where abusers deflect responsibility by making the survivor feel at fault for their actions, leading to confusion, self-blame and even efforts to "fix" the relationship *(domesticshelters.org)*

Breadcrumbing: Also called Hansel and Grettelling, the practice of sporadically feigning interest in another person in order to keep them interested, despite lacking genuine investment in the relationship *(wikipedia.com)*

Coercive Control: A pattern of acts and behaviors that an abuser uses to take away your freedom and to control your life. The abuser may use fear, pressure, shame, or rules to wear you down and take over your choices *(www.womenslaw.org)*

Cognitive Dissonance: Anxiety or discomfort that results from simultaneously holding contradictory or otherwise incompatible attitudes, beliefs, or the like, such as when someone likes a person but disapproves strongly of one of their habits *(dictionary.com)*

Gaslighting: The use of psychological manipulation to undermine a person's faith in their own judgment, memory, or sanity.

The practice of deceiving people through the repetition of a constructed false narrative *(dictionary.com)*

Grey Rock Method: A communication pattern to deliberately act unresponsive and uninterested to encourage disengagement with difficult people *(wikipedia.com)*

Hoovering: A term used to describe a set of behaviors that a person uses to manipulate others back into a toxic relationship with them *(psychcentral.com)*

Love Bombing: The action or practice of lavishing someone with attention or affection, especially in order to influence or manipulate them *(dictionary.com)*

Narcissistic Projection: A defense mechanism where a person with narcissistic traits disowns their negative feelings, flaws, or unacceptable behaviors and attributes them onto another person *(choosingtherapy.com)*

Reactive Abuse: When a victim of abuse becomes aggressive toward their abuser. It's a defensive reaction to experiencing ongoing and sustained abuse *(GoodRx.com)*

Red Flag: A metaphor of a sign of some particular problem requiring attention *(wikipedia.com)*

Smear Campaign: Also referred to as a smear tactic or simply a smear, it is an effort to damage or call into question someone's reputation *(wikipedia.com)*

Trauma Bond: Emotional bonds that arise from a cyclical pattern of abuse. Occurring in an abusive relationship, the victim forms an emotional connection with the perpetrator *(wikipedia.com)*

Triangulation: When a toxic or manipulative person, often a person with strong narcissistic traits, brings a third person into their relationship in order to remain in control *(psychcentral.com)*

Word Salad: A tactic used to manipulate, confuse or overwhelm a listener during an argument, designed to avoid responsibility, gaslight, and deflect

Traits of a Covert Narcissist

- VERY INSECURE
- SNEAKY AND MANIPULATIVE
- EXHIBITS PASSIVE-AGGRESSIVE BEHAVIOR
- EXCEEDINGLY JEALOUS OF OTHERS
- PLAYS THE VICTIM
- FAKES A HUMBLE DEMEANOR
- HAS INCONSISTENT PUBLIC AND PRIVATE LIVES
- HOLDS GRUDGES
- CANNOT ADMIT MISTAKES
- HIGHLY SENSITIVE TO CRITICISM
- HAS GRANDIOSE AND UNATTAINABLE FANTASIES
- PRONE TO DEPRESSION
- SEES THEMSELVES AS SUPERIOR TO OTHERS
- LACKS EMPATHY
- HAS AN EXCESSIVE NEED FOR ADMIRATION

Resources

For immediate help, contact the National Domestic Violence Hotline, available 24/7, confidentially
thehotline.org
1800-799-SAFE

To find a shelter near you visit
domesticshelters.org

To find a therapist in your area visit
betterhelp.com

To connect with Mia Hanks visit
www.miajhanks.com

About The Author

Mia Hanks is the author of *Bride-Made: A Memoir.* She resides in the Midwest where she enjoys writing and running a small crafting business. A graduate of Vanderbilt University, Mia is also the proud mom of two very creative adult children and one highly enthusiastic rescue dog. Music has always been her passion, though these days it competes with crochet hooks and yarn. *I've Made Plans* is her second book.

NOTES

www.ingramcontent.com/pod-product-compliance
Lightning Source LLC
LaVergne TN
LVHW010935110826
845149LV00013B/2614